D0623480

The
Wish-Bone

DRESSING

Cookbook

SMITHMARK

This edition published in 1991 by Ottenheimer Publishers, Inc. for SMITHMARK Publishers Inc., 112 Madison Avenue, New York, NY 10016.

SMITHMARK books are available for bulk purchase for sales promotion and premium use. For details write or telephone the Manager of Special Sales, SMITHMARK Publishers Inc., 112 Madison Avenue, New York, NY 10016. (212) 532-6600.

Contents

Introduction

Wish-Bone® Dressings are as versatile as they are flavorful. They not only enhance the taste of hot and cold salads, but are also indispensable as tenderizers and seasonings in appetizers, meat and seafood dishes, vegetables, sauces, and sandwiches.

This cookbook introduces you to Wish-Bone cookery with a tantalizing array of recipes, all using delicious Wish-Bone Dressings. You'll find recipes for appetizers, hot entrees, glazes and sauces, vegetables, relishes, breads, sandwiches, and of course, salads. Dressings such as Wish-Bone Italian, Russian, or Sweet 'n Spicy French add flavor to dishes, are great marinades, and are a delicious alternative to oil when sautéing and stir frying.

All the recipes have been taste tested in The Lipton Kitchens by a professional staff of home economists. The easy-to-follow directions assure perfect results each time. Many of the recipes are accompanied by beautiful full-color photographs.

You'll find that Wish-Bone Dressings bring new and exciting accents to your cooking!

Appetizers

Banderillas *20 appetizers*

*1 pound shrimp, cleaned and cooked
(about 20)*
*2 cans (14 ounces each) artichoke
hearts, drained and halved, or 2
packages (9 ounces each) frozen
artichoke hearts, cooked and drained*

*¾ cup Wish-Bone® Italian
Dressing*
¼ cup finely chopped parsley

In shallow dish, combine all ingredients. Cover and marinate in refrigerator, turning occasionally, 4 hours or overnight. To serve, skewer shrimp and artichokes on wooden skewers or toothpicks.

Yakitori *24 appetizers*

*⅓ cup Wish-Bone Sweet 'n Spicy
French Dressing*
2 tablespoons soy sauce
*2 tablespoons Japanese rice wine or
dry sherry*
¼ cup sugar

*2 whole chicken breasts (1 pound each),
skinned, boned, and cut into
¾-inch cubes*
*Green onion fans or green pepper
chunks*

In medium shallow baking dish, blend dressing, soy sauce, wine, and sugar; add chicken. Cover and marinate in refrigerator, turning occasionally, at least 2 hours. Remove chicken, reserving marinade. On small skewers or wooden toothpicks, thread chicken and green onions. Broil, turning and basting frequently with reserved marinade, until done. (See photo, page 13.)

Sesame Beef Sticks   *25 appetizers*

½ cup Wish-Bone *Italian Dressing*
3 tablespoons sugar
1 tablespoon soy sauce

1 pound boneless sirloin or round steak,
*   cut into thin 3-inch strips*
Sesame seeds

In large shallow baking dish, blend all ingredients except beef and sesame seeds; add beef. Cover and marinate in refrigerator, turning occasionally, at least 2 hours. Remove beef and thread on small skewers, reserving marinade. Roll beef in sesame seeds; broil, turning once and spooning on reserved marinade, until done.

Stuffed Clams Normandy   *4 servings*

12 clams, scrubbed
¼ cup Wish-Bone *Italian Dressing*
⅔ cup dry bread crumbs
2 tablespoons finely chopped parsley

2 tablespoons diced drained pimiento
2 tablespoons grated Parmesan cheese
¼ cup warm water
Rock or coarse salt (optional)

Preheat oven to 350°F. In large saucepan, place clams and enough water to cover bottom of saucepan. Cover and steam clams over high heat until shells open, about 8 minutes. (Discard any that do not open.) Remove and chop clams finely; reserve and wash 12 half shells. In medium bowl, combine clams, dressing, bread crumbs, parsley, pimiento, cheese, and warm water. Heap mixture into reserved clam shells. In shallow baking pan, place ½-inch layer of salt; arrange shells on top. Bake 20 minutes, then place under broiler to brown.

Londonderry Watercress Rounds   *60 appetizers*

½ cup butter or margarine, softened
¼ cup Wish-Bone *Ranch Dressing*

1 cup chopped watercress
30 slices thin-sliced white bread

In small bowl, blend butter and dressing; add watercress. Using 1½-inch biscuit cutter, cut 120 rounds from bread. Cut ½-inch circle from center of half the rounds to form "doughnut" shape. Spread remaining rounds with dressing mixture, then top with "doughnut" rounds. Wrap in waxed paper or plastic wrap and chill. Garnish, if desired, with sprig of watercress in center of each. (See photo, page 15.)

Yakitori (page 11), Sesame Beef Sticks, Stuffed Clams Normandy

Holiday Cocktail Cheese Ball *3½ cups*

A perfect hostess gift at any time of the year. Take one along with you to assure your welcome.

1 cup shredded Cheddar cheese (about 4 ounces)
2 packages (4 ounces each) blue cheese, crumbled
½ cup Wish-Bone Thousand Island Dressing

1 hard-cooked egg, chopped
2 tablespoons diced green pepper
2 teaspoons Worcestershire sauce
⅛ teaspoon hot pepper sauce
1 cup chopped pimiento-stuffed olives

In medium bowl, combine all ingredients except olives; chill until firm. Shape into ball and roll in olives.

Nutty Cream Cheese Spirals *60 appetizers*

⅔ cup Wish-Bone Russian Dressing
1 package (8 ounces) cream cheese, softened

1 cup finely chopped walnuts
1 loaf (16 ounces) white bread, cut into 8 lengthwise slices

In medium bowl, combine all ingredients except bread. Trim crusts from bread; flatten slightly with rolling pin. Spread 3 tablespoons dressing mixture on each slice of bread; roll jelly-roll style. Wrap in waxed paper or plastic wrap and chill. To serve, cut into ½-inch slices.

Simply Smashing Ham Ribbons *72 appetizers*

¼ cup Wish-Bone Deluxe French or Sweet 'n Spicy French Dressing
¼ cup apricot preserves
⅛ teaspoon dry mustard
Softened butter

1 loaf thin-sliced white bread, crusts trimmed (about 24 slices)
1 loaf thin-sliced whole wheat bread, crusts trimmed (about 24 slices)
12 thin slices cooked ham

In small bowl, blend dressing, preserves, and mustard. For each of 12 sandwich stacks, layer as follows: buttered white bread; whole wheat bread spread with 2 teaspoons dressing mixture; unbuttered white bread; ham slice; buttered whole wheat bread, buttered side down. Wrap in waxed paper or plastic wrap and chill. To serve, cut each stack into thirds lengthwise, then in half crosswise.

Simply Smashing Ham Ribbons, Londonderry Watercress Rounds (page 12),
Stuffed Mushrooms Caesar (page 16), Nutty Cream Cheese Spirals

Stuffed Mushrooms Caesar   *24 appetizers*

1 pound large fresh mushrooms
¼ cup Wish-Bone *Olive Oil Classics*
  Caesar Dressing

1 cup fresh bread crumbs
¼ cup grated Parmesan cheese
1 tablespoon finely chopped parsley

Preheat oven to 350°F. Remove and finely chop mushroom stems. In medium bowl, combine dressing, bread crumbs, cheese, parsley, and chopped stems. Fill each mushroom cap with bread crumb mixture; place in shallow baking dish. Add water to barely cover bottom and bake 20 minutes. Serve hot or cold. (See photo, page 15.)

Deluxe Pear Salad   *4 to 8 servings*

1 cup (8 ounces) creamed cottage cheese
¼ cup thinly sliced celery
¼ cup coarsely chopped walnuts
8 canned or fresh pear halves

Lettuce leaves
¼ cup Wish-Bone *Deluxe French*
  Dressing

In small bowl, combine cottage cheese, celery, and walnuts. Arrange pear halves on lettuce; fill with cheese mixture. Spoon dressing over pears.

Pasta Antipasto   *8 servings*

½ pound rotelle macaroni, ziti, or
  medium shell macaroni
1 cup (8 ounces) Wish-Bone
  Italian Dressing
1 cup sliced mushrooms
1 cup pitted ripe olives
½ cup roasted red pepper, cut
  into strips

Lettuce leaves
3 medium tomatoes, sliced
3 hard-cooked eggs, sliced
1 cup cooked artichoke hearts, halved
¼ cup thinly sliced salami or pepperoni
¼ cup provolone or mozzarella cheese,
  cut into strips

Cook macaroni according to package directions; drain and rinse with cold water until completely cool. In large bowl, combine ⅔ cup dressing, mushrooms, olives, and red pepper. Add macaroni and toss well. On large, lettuce-lined platter, arrange macaroni mixture, tomatoes, eggs, artichokes, salami, and cheese; chill. Just before serving, drizzle with remaining dressing.

Pasta Antipasto

Side Dish Salads

Waldorf Slaw *14 servings*

5 cups shredded cabbage
2 cups diced apple
1/3 cup raisins

1/2 cup·mayonnaise
1/4 cup Wish-Bone Sweet 'n Spicy
French Dressing

In large bowl, combine cabbage, diced apple, and raisins; toss with mayonnaise and dressing.

Simply Dilly Cucumbers *24 cucumber spears*

1/2 cup Wish-Bone Italian or Lite
Italian Dressing
1/2 cup sour cream
2 tablespoons chopped fresh dill or
1 teaspoon dried dill weed

4 medium cucumbers, peeled and sliced
into spears (about 1 1/2 pounds)

In small bowl, blend dressing, sour cream, and dill. Lay cucumber spears in large covered container, add dressing mixture; toss. Secure cover tightly and chill, tossing spears occasionally, 4 hours or overnight. Store in refrigerator for up to 1 week.

Speedy Potato Salad *10 servings*

*3 cans (16 ounces each) sliced potatoes,
   drained and rinsed
1 cup sliced celery*

*2 tablespoons chopped onion
½ cup sour cream
¼ cup* Wish-Bone *Italian Dressing*

In bowl, combine potatoes, celery, and onion; toss with sour cream blended with dressing and chill.

Perky Picnic Bean Salad *4 to 6 servings*

A cool, crunchy way to serve baked beans.

*1 can (16 ounces) pork and beans in
   tomato sauce
1 cup sliced celery*

*1 cup coarsely chopped green pepper
1 tablespoon molasses*
Wish-Bone *Italian Dressing*

In large bowl, combine all ingredients except dressing. Toss with ¼ to ½ cup dressing, depending on consistency desired; chill.

Unique Summer Salads *1 cup dressing*

Wish-Bone Italian Dressing gives mayonnaise added zest in any salad.

All-in-One Dressing

½ cup Wish-Bone *Italian or Lite Italian
   Dressing*

½ cup mayonnaise

In small bowl, blend all ingredients; chill.

Tasty Potato Salad: In large bowl, combine 4 cooked cubed potatoes (about 2 pounds), 1 cup sliced celery, and ¼ cup chopped onion; toss with All-in-One Dressing and chill.

Perfect Pasta Salad: In large bowl, combine 4 cups cooked macaroni or egg noodles, ½ cup chopped red or green pepper, and ½ cup chopped onion; toss with All-in-One Dressing and chill.

Perky Rice Salad: In large bowl, combine 3 cups cooked rice, 1 cup chopped tomato, and ¼ cup sliced green onions; toss with All-in-One Dressing and chill.

Super Slaw: In large bowl, combine 4 cups shredded raw cabbage, 1 cup shredded carrot, and ¼ cup chopped onion; toss with All-in-One Dressing and chill.

Garden Gazpacho Salad *8 servings*

1 cup (8 ounces) Wish-Bone *Robusto
   Italian, Italian, Lite Italian,
   or Blended Italian Dressing*
¼ cup tomato juice
6 dashes hot pepper sauce (optional)
2 medium cucumbers, chopped

2 medium tomatoes, chopped
2 medium green peppers, chopped
1 medium onion, chopped
*1 loaf unsliced round bread (about 9
   inches diameter)*
Lettuce leaves

In large bowl, blend dressing, tomato juice, and hot pepper sauce. Stir in vegetables. Cover and marinate in refrigerator, stirring occasionally, at least 2 hours. Cut lengthwise slice off top of bread. Hollow out center, leaving ½-inch shell. Just before serving, line bread shell with lettuce and fill with vegetable mixture. To serve, spoon out vegetable mixture, then cut bread shell into wedges.

Fall Festival Mixed Salad *6 to 8 servings*

Mixed salad greens
3 cups uncooked broccoli florets
3 cups uncooked cauliflower florets
2 cups sliced zucchini

¼ pound fresh mushrooms, sliced
1 cup (8 ounces) Wish-Bone *Italian
   Dressing*
⅓ cup crumbled crisp-cooked bacon

In large salad bowl, combine salad greens, broccoli, cauliflower, zucchini, and mushrooms; chill. Just before serving, toss with dressing and bacon.

Italian Confetti Salad *4 to 6 servings*

*1 can (16 ounces) cut green beans,
   drained*
1 jar (16 ounces) sliced carrots, drained

*1 can (16 ounces) whole kernel corn,
   drained*
2 tablespoons finely chopped onion
¾ cup Wish-Bone *Italian Dressing*

In large bowl, combine all ingredients; cover and chill. Serve on salad greens.

Fruit Promenade   *4 servings*

4 large pears
3 tablespoons Wish-Bone *Russian or*
  Lite Russian Dressing
1 tablespoon honey

¾ cup halved grapes
1 banana, sliced
¼ cup shredded coconut

Cut thin slice lengthwise from side of pears and remove pulp, leaving ¼-inch shell to form cups. Reserve ½ cup chopped pulp. (Save remaining pear pulp to use in a fresh fruit salad.) In medium bowl, blend dressing and honey. Add reserved ½ cup pulp, grapes, banana, and coconut; toss thoroughly. Spoon into pear cups; wrap and chill.

Italian Tomato Salad Topping   *4 cups topping*

Toss this colorful mixture with greens for instant salad.

2 cups coarsely chopped tomato
1 cup chopped red onion
1 cup diagonally sliced celery
½ cup Wish-Bone *Italian or Lite Italian*
  Dressing

2 tablespoons dry red wine
1 tablespoon chopped fresh basil or 1
  teaspoon dry basil

In large bowl, combine tomato, onion, and celery; add dressing blended with wine and basil. Spoon into 1-quart jar; secure lid tightly and chill, inverting jar occasionally, 4 hours or overnight. Store in refrigerator for up to 1 week.

Buona Festa Platter   *8 to 10 servings*

A beautiful example of canned vegetables in a colorful and tasty salad.

2 cups (16 ounces) Wish-Bone *Italian*
  Dressing
1 can (16 ounces) whole green beans,
  drained
1 can (14 ounces) whole artichoke
  hearts, drained and halved (optional)

1 can (15 ounces) asparagus spears,
  drained
1 can (8¼ ounces) whole beets, drained
1 can (8 ounces) sliced carrots, drained
1 can (4 ounces) whole mushrooms,
  drained

Marinate *each* vegetable in a separate bowl as follows: pour ½ cup dressing over green beans and artichoke hearts; pour ¼ cup over asparagus, beets, carrots, and mushrooms. Cover and marinate in refrigerator, turning occasionally, 4 hours or overnight. To serve, arrange vegetables on platter.

Main Dish Salads

Salade Niçoise à la Wish-Bone   *4 servings*

Mixed salad greens
4 cups sliced cooked potatoes (about 6
  medium)
3 cups cooked cut-up green beans
  (about ¾ pound)
1 can (9¼ ounces) chunk tuna, drained
4 hard-cooked eggs, quartered

2 medium tomatoes, cut into wedges
½ cup pitted ripe olives
1 can (2 ounces) anchovy fillets
1 cup (8 ounces) Wish-Bone *Sweet 'n*
  Spicy French or Deluxe French
  Dressing

On serving platter, arrange salad greens, potatoes, green beans, tuna, eggs, tomatoes, olives, and anchovies; chill. Just before serving, pour dressing over salad.

Fisherman's Favorite Cioppino Salad   *6 servings*

1 cup (8 ounces)
  Wish-Bone Italian Dressing
¼ cup dry white wine
¾ teaspoon chopped fresh basil leaves
  or ¼ teaspoon dried basil leaves
2 cups cooked crabmeat (about
  ¾ pound)
¾ pound large shrimp, cleaned and
  cooked

Mixed salad greens
3 medium tomatoes, coarsely chopped
10 artichoke hearts, halved, or 1 can
  (15 ounces) artichoke hearts, drained
  and halved
1 medium red onion, cut into rings

In large shallow baking dish, blend dressing, wine, and basil; add crabmeat and shrimp. Cover and marinate in refrigerator, stirring occasionally, at least 2 hours. Meanwhile, in large salad bowl, arrange salad greens, tomatoes, artichoke hearts, and onion; cover and chill. Just before serving, add seafood with marinade and toss. Garnish, if desired, with chopped parsley.

Dilly of a Deli Salad   *6 servings*

A tangy do-ahead salad that is a cinch to serve.

1/3 cup Wish-Bone *Italian Dressing*
3/4 cup mayonnaise
4 cups thinly sliced cooked potatoes or 3
    cans (16 ounces each) sliced
    potatoes, drained
3/4 pound cold meats, cut into 1/2-inch
    cubes (salami, ham, turkey, corned
    beef, roast beef, bologna, etc.)

1/2 pound assorted cheeses, shredded
    (American, Cheddar, Swiss,
    Muenster, brick, etc.)
1 medium tomato, coarsely chopped and
    drained
1/2 cup chopped dill pickle spears
Dill pickle spears (optional)

In large bowl, blend dressing with mayonnaise; add potatoes, cold meats, cheeses, tomato, and pickles. Toss until coated. Pack into an 8-inch springform pan and chill 4 hours or overnight. Garnish, if desired, with dill pickle spears.

Garden Green
Chicken Salad Mold   *8 servings*

2 envelopes Knox *Unflavored Gelatine*
2 cups cold water
1 cup boiling water
2 tablespoons lemon juice
2 tablespoons sugar
2 teaspoons salt
1/2 cup Wish-Bone *Olive Oil Classics*
    Caesar Dressing

Assorted garnishes (sliced olives,
    pimiento strips, cucumber slices,
    tomato wedges or slices, green pepper
    rings, or cherry tomatoes)
2 cups shredded cooked chicken
1/2 cup thinly diagonally sliced celery
1/2 cup diced cucumber
1/4 cup diced green pepper

In medium bowl, sprinkle unflavored gelatine over 1 cup cold water; let stand 1 minute. Add boiling water and stir until gelatine is completely dissolved. Add lemon juice, sugar, salt, dressing, and remaining water. Pour 1/4 cup gelatine mixture into 6-cup mold. Arrange garnishes in bottom of mold; chill until set. Chill remaining gelatine, stirring occasionally, until mixture is consistency of unbeaten egg whites. Fold in chicken, celery, cucumber, and green pepper. Gently pour mixture onto garnish layer and chill until firm. Unmold onto lettuce-lined serving platter.

Dilly of a Deli Salad

Sensational Salad Compose *4 servings*

3 medium potatoes, peeled and cut into strips (about 3" × ½")
2 tablespoons chopped parsley
1 cup (8 ounces) Wish-Bone *Lite Italian Dressing*
4 medium beets or 1 can (16 ounces) sliced beets, drained
¼ pound spinach leaves
¾ pound sliced roast beef
1 small red onion, peeled and thinly sliced

In medium saucepan, boil potatoes in salted water 6 minutes or until tender. Drain and rinse in cold water; pat dry. In medium bowl, combine potatoes, parsley, and ⅓ cup dressing. Cover and marinate in refrigerator, turning occasionally, at least 4 hours. Meanwhile, preheat oven to 400°F. Wrap beets in aluminum foil and bake 50 minutes or until tender. Let cool; peel and cut into thin slices. To serve, line serving platter with spinach leaves, then arrange beets, potato mixture, roast beef, and onion in a decorative pattern. Serve with remaining dressing.

"End of a Sunny Day" Salad *4 servings*

Once you've tasted rice salad you'll be hooked. And it's such a creative way to transform humble leftovers into gourmet fare.

3 cups cooked rice
1 cup (8 ounces) Wish-Bone *Russian or Lite Russian Dressing*
¼ cup finely chopped green onions
1 can (8 ounces) pineapple chunks in natural juice, drained (reserve 1 tablespoon juice)
1 tablespoon soy sauce
¾ teaspoon ground ginger
2 cups cubed cooked chicken, turkey, beef, or pork
2 medium green peppers, cut into 1-inch chunks
1 can (8½ ounces) water chestnuts, drained and sliced

In medium bowl, combine rice, ⅓ cup dressing, green onions, and reserved pineapple juice. Pack into lightly greased 3- or 4-cup ring mold; chill. In medium bowl, combine remaining dressing, soy sauce, and ginger. Add chicken, green peppers, pineapple, and water chestnuts; chill, tossing occasionally, at least 2 hours. To serve, unmold rice ring and fill center with salad mixture. Serve, if desired, on fresh lettuce or spinach leaves.

Sensational Salad Compose

Rush Hour Supper Platter   *4 servings*

Mixed salad greens
2 cans (16 ounces each) sliced potatoes,
    drained, or 3 cups sliced cooked
    potatoes
1 can (16 ounces) cut green beans,
    drained, or 2 cups cooked cut green
    beans

2 medium tomatoes, cut into wedges
2 cans (7 ounces each) tuna, drained
½ cup pitted ripe olives
½ cup roasted red pepper, cut into strips
1 can (2 ounces) anchovies, drained
¾ cup Wish-Bone *Robusto Italian or
    Italian Dressing*

On serving platter, arrange all ingredients except dressing. Just before serving, drizzle with dressing.

Thousand Island Chicken Salad   *4 servings*

½ cup Wish-Bone *Thousand Island or
    Lite Thousand Island Dressing*
2 cups shredded cooked chicken

½ cup diced celery
¼ cup coarsely chopped walnuts
Salt and pepper to taste

In large bowl, combine all ingredients; chill. Serve, if desired, on lettuce or as a sandwich spread.

Gala Salad Toss   *6 servings*

Just right for a cool summer luncheon. Serve with iced tea and fruit.

1 medium head iceberg lettuce, torn
    into pieces
1 tomato, cut into wedges
1 green pepper, diced
3 green onions, sliced

1 cup cut-up cooked turkey or chicken
½ cup sliced celery
1 cup seasoned croutons
½ cup Wish-Bone *Chunky Blue Cheese
    or Lite Chunky Blue Cheese Dressing*

In salad bowl, arrange lettuce, tomato, green pepper, green onions, turkey, and celery; chill. Just before serving, toss with croutons and dressing.

Rush Hour Supper Platter

Wild Rice and Seafood Salad *6 servings*

1/2 cup Wish-Bone Creamy Italian, Lite Creamy Italian, or Lite Thousand Island Dressing

1 pound medium shrimp, cleaned, cooked, and coarsely chopped, or 2 packages (6 ounces each) frozen crabmeat, thawed and drained (Increase dressing to 3/4 cup.)

2 cups cooked wild or regular white rice

1 small red or green pepper, chopped

1/2 cup halved seedless grapes

1/4 cup sliced almonds, toasted

1 teaspoon lemon juice

3 dashes hot pepper sauce

Lettuce leaves

Lemon slices (optional)

In large bowl, combine all ingredients except lettuce; cover and chill. To serve, line bowl or individual serving dishes with lettuce; fill with shrimp mixture. Garnish, if desired, with lemon slices.

Tuna Deluxe Salad *6 servings*

1 small head iceberg lettuce, torn into pieces

1/2 head romaine lettuce, torn into pieces

2 cans (7 ounces each) tuna, drained and flaked

1/2 pound fresh mushrooms, sliced

2 tomatoes, cut into wedges

1 green pepper, cut into rings

3/4 cup Wish-Bone Italian, Lite Italian, or Deluxe French Dressing

In salad bowl, arrange lettuces, tuna, mushrooms, tomatoes, and green pepper; chill. Just before serving, toss with dressing.

Buttons 'n Bows *4 servings*

1 package (8 ounces) egg noddle bows

3/4 cup Wish-Bone Thousand Island Dressing

1 cup thinly sliced celery

1/2 cup sliced pimiento-stuffed olives

1/4 cup finely chopped onion

1 hard-cooked egg, chopped

Cook noodles according to package directions; drain and rinse with cold water until completely cool. In large bowl, combine dressing, noodles, celery, olives, onion, and egg; chill.

Wild Rice and Seafood Salad

Hot Entrees

Italian Steak and Vegetables *6 servings*

1 cup (8 ounces) Wish-Bone *Italian or
  Lite Italian Dressing*
*2-pound boneless chuck steak, 1 inch
  thick*
1 can (16 ounces) whole tomatoes

1 pound fresh green beans
*1 medium eggplant, cut into ½-inch
  slices*
1 pound fresh mushrooms, sliced

In shallow baking dish, pour ½ cup dressing over beef; cover and marinate in
refrigerator, turning occasionally, at least 3 hours. Repeat procedure with remaining dressing and vegetables. In large skillet, brown beef; add beef marinade and
simmer covered 45 minutes. Add tomatoes, beans, and vegetable marinade and
continue simmering, covered, 40 minutes. Add eggplant and simmer covered 20
minutes. During last 10 minutes of cooking, add mushrooms.

Sukiyaki Skillet *6 to 8 servings*

¾ cup Wish-Bone *Russian Dressing*
2 tablespoons soy sauce
2 tablespoons brown sugar
*1½ pounds boneless sirloin or flank
  steak, cut into thin strips*

2 tablespoons cornstarch
*4 cups combined vegetables (sliced
  celery, green onions, mushrooms,
  water chestnuts, bamboo shoots, fresh
  spinach, or bean sprouts)*

In large shallow baking dish, blend dressing, soy sauce, and brown sugar; add beef.
Cover and marinate in refrigerator, turning occasionally, at least 2 hours. Remove
beef, reserving marinade; toss with cornstarch. In large skillet, brown beef over
high heat. Add combined vegetables and cook, stirring constantly, 2 minutes or
until vegetables are tender. Add reserved marinade and heat through. Serve, if
desired, over rice.

Stuffed Green Peppers Parmesan   *6 servings*

6 large green peppers
½ cup Wish-Bone *Italian Dressing*
½ cup chopped onion
1½ pounds ground beef
1 cup cooked rice
½ cup dry bread crumbs

¼ cup grated Parmesan cheese
2 tablespoons chopped parsley
2 eggs, well beaten
1 can (8 ounces) tomato sauce
¼ cup water

Preheat oven to 350°F. Wash peppers; remove stems and seeds; parboil in salted water. Drain. In large skillet, heat ¼ cup dressing and cook onion until tender. Add ground beef and brown well. Stir in rice and allow mixture to cool slightly. Stir bread crumbs, cheese, parsley, and eggs into meat mixture. Stuff peppers with mixture. Place in greased baking dish. In small bowl, combine remaining dressing with tomato sauce and water. Pour over peppers. Bake 20 minutes or until tender.

Simply Delicious Skewered Steak   *4 servings*

¾ cup Wish-Bone *Italian or Russian Dressing*
1½ pounds steak (your favorite cut), cut into 1½-inch cubes

Assorted vegetables (fresh mushrooms, green pepper chunks, cherry tomatoes, and onions)

In large shallow baking dish, pour dressing over steak and vegetables. Cover and marinate in refrigerator at least 3 hours, turning occasionally. On skewers, alternately thread steak and vegetables. Grill or broil until done, turning and basting frequently with remaining marinade.

Mock Sauerbraten   *8 servings*

1 cup (8 ounces) Wish-Bone *Italian Dressing*
1½ cups water
6 bay leaves
10 whole cloves

4 whole black peppers
⅛ teaspoon ground ginger
4-pound beef rump roast
⅔ cup crumbled ginger snaps

In large bowl, combine dressing, 1 cup water, bay leaves, cloves, peppers, and ginger. Add meat, turning to coat; cover and marinate in refrigerator about 24 hours. In large saucepan or Dutch oven, brown meat; add marinade. Simmer covered 2 hours or until meat is tender. Strain marinade into medium saucepan and combine with remaining water and ginger snaps. Cook, stirring constantly, until smooth.

Glazed Corned Beef   *4 to 6 servings*

An easy way to produce a dinner that has as much zap as it has good looks.

½ cup Wish-Bone *Russian Dressing*
2 tablespoons brown sugar
1 tablespoon prepared mustard
1 teaspoon prepared horseradish

½ teaspoon Worcestershire sauce
½ teaspoon ground cloves
3- to 4-pound cooked corned beef

Preheat oven to 350°F. In small bowl, combine dressing, brown sugar, mustard, horseradish, Worcestershire, and cloves. In shallow baking pan, place meat, fat side up; score if desired. Brush glaze over meat; bake about 20 minutes. Heat remaining glaze and serve over meat. (See photo, page 41.)

Marinated Steak   *8 servings*

½ cup Wish-Bone *Italian, Robusto Italian, or Lite Italian Dressing*

2-pound flank, London broil, sirloin, or chuck steak

In large shallow baking dish, pour dressing over steak. Cover and marinate in refrigerator, turning occasionally, at least 4 hours. Remove steak, reserving marinade. Grill or broil steak, basting frequently with reserved marinade, until done.

Rain or Shine Barbecue   *8 servings*

1 cup (8 ounces) Wish-Bone *Russian or Sweet 'n Spicy French Dressing*
1 jar (12 ounces) apricot preserves
1 envelope Lipton® *Onion Recipe Soup Mix*

3 pounds spareribs, cut into serving pieces
2½- to 3-pound chicken, cut into serving pieces

In medium bowl, blend dressing, preserves, and Lipton Onion Soup Mix; set aside.

Indoors: Preheat oven to 375°F. In large shallow baking pan, bake spareribs 30 minutes. Then begin to bake chicken, arranged in separate large shallow baking pan. Brush chicken and spareribs with half the glaze; bake 30 minutes. Brush with remaining glaze, then bake an additional 15 minutes or until chicken and spareribs are done.

Outdoors: Grill spareribs 30 minutes. Then, add chicken and grill 20 minutes. Brush chicken and spareribs with glaze and continue to grill, turning and basting frequently, until chicken and spareribs are done.

Hawaiian Islands Luau   *6 servings*

1 cup (8 ounces) Wish-Bone *Sweet 'n Spicy French Dressing*
½ cup peach preserves
1 tablespoon soy sauce
2 pounds spareribs, cut into individual ribs and parboiled

6 chicken legs (about 1½ pounds)
Sliced bananas, peaches, pears, limes, or pineapple chunks
Shredded coconut

Preheat oven to 375°F. In small bowl, combine dressing, preserves, and soy sauce. In foil-lined jelly-roll pan, bake spareribs 30 minutes; drain. Add chicken and bake, basting both spareribs and chicken frequently with 1¼ cups dressing glaze, 45 minutes or until chicken is tender. Meanwhile, alternately thread assorted fruit on 6 small skewers. Bake, basting frequently with remaining glaze, 10 minutes; roll in coconut. Serve with spareribs and chicken.

Rain or Shine Barbecue

No-Carve Stuffed Pork Roast *6 servings*

A festive way to serve a roast and avoid last-minute carving.

*6 double pork loin chops (about 3
 pounds)*
½ cup Wish-Bone *Russian Dressing*
1 cup dry bread crumbs
*1 can (7 ounces) whole kernel corn,
 drained*

*1 can (4 ounces) sliced mushrooms,
 drained*
¼ cup finely chopped green pepper
Salt and pepper to taste
⅔ cup water

Preheat oven to 350°F. Cut a deep pocket in each chop for stuffing. Brush inside of pockets with ¼ cup dressing. In large shallow roasting pan, pour remaining dressing over chops; marinate ½ hour, turning once. In medium bowl, combine bread crumbs, corn, mushrooms, green pepper, salt, and pepper. Equally divide mixture among chops; stuff. Stand chops upright, one against the other, in the marinade pan and secure with long skewer. Pour water around chops; cover tightly with foil and bake 1 hour. Remove foil and bake an additional 30 minutes or until chops are done.

Pork Sukiyaki *6 to 8 servings*

¼ cup soy sauce
¼ cup water
2 tablespoons sugar
½ cup Wish-Bone *Italian Dressing*
2 pounds pork loin, sliced paper thin
1 cup sliced celery

*2 cans (5 ounces each) bamboo shoots,
 drained*
*1 can (4 ounces) sliced mushrooms,
 drained*
1 cup sliced green onions

In small bowl, combine soy sauce, water, and sugar. In large skillet, heat dressing and brown meat well. Push meat to one side of skillet; pour half of soy mixture over meat. To other side of skillet, add celery, bamboo shoots, and mushrooms. Simmer 8 to 10 minutes. Add green onions and cover vegetables with remaining soy mixture. Cook an additional 5 minutes.

Rib-Sticking Good Spareribs *4 servings*

1 cup (8 ounces) Wish-Bone *Russian Dressing*

3½ pounds spareribs, cut into serving pieces and parboiled
½ cup maple syrup

In large shallow baking dish, pour dressing over spareribs. Cover and marinate in refrigerator, turning occasionally, at least 3 hours. Preheat oven to 375°F. Remove ribs, reserving marinade. Place ribs on rack in foil-lined baking dish. Bake, turning once and basting frequently with reserved marinade blended with maple syrup, 30 minutes or until ribs are done.

Glazed Ham Steak *6 servings*

½ cup Wish-Bone *Russian or Deluxe French Dressing*
¼ cup brown sugar

1 tablespoon prepared mustard
1½- to 2-pound cooked ham steak, about 1 inch thick

In small bowl, blend dressing, sugar, and mustard. Place ham on broiler rack and spread with dressing mixture. Broil 3 inches from heat for about 20 minutes, turning once and basting frequently with remaining dressing mixture, until glazed.

Mandarin-Stuffed Ham Grill *4 servings*

¾ cup Wish-Bone *Russian Dressing*
2 cooked ham steaks (¾ to 1 pound each) about ½ inch thick
1 can (11 ounces) mandarin oranges, drained and chopped

1 can (8¼ ounces) crushed pineapple, drained
¾ cup plain toasted croutons
⅓ cup raisins
⅓ cup brown sugar

In shallow baking dish, pour dressing over ham; cover and marinate in refrigerator, turning occasionally, at least 3 hours. In medium saucepan, combine oranges, pineapple, croutons, raisins, and sugar; heat through. Place stuffing mixture on one steak and top with remaining steak; tie securely with string. Grill or broil 10 minutes, turning once and basting with remaining marinade.

Glazed Corned Beef (page 34)

Elegantly Stuffed Fish   *6 to 8 servings*

¾ cup Wish-Bone *Creamy Italian
  Dressing*
½ cup chopped green pepper
½ cup chopped onion
1⅓ cups dry bread crumbs
1 cup flaked crabmeat (about 6 ounces)

½ cup sliced almonds
¼ cup lemon juice
3- to 4-pound dressed whole fish
1 tablespoon white wine or lemon juice
4 tomatoes, halved
Lemon slices (optional)

Preheat oven to 350°F. In medium skillet, heat ¼ cup dressing and cook green pepper and onion until tender. Remove from heat and stir in 1 cup bread crumbs, crabmeat, almonds, lemon juice, and ¼ cup dressing. Stuff fish; secure opening with thread. Place in greased shallow baking pan and brush with 2 tablespoons dressing blended with wine; bake 15 minutes. Meanwhile, combine remaining bread crumbs and 2 tablespoons dressing; spoon onto tomato halves. Place tomatoes in casserole around fish. Bake an additional 30 minutes or until fish flakes. Garnish, if desired, with lemon slices.

Fisherman's Casserole   *4 to 6 servings*

A dressed-up meal for guests, yet easy to prepare and serve. Vegetable salad is a crispy complement.

3 tablespoons butter or margarine
¼ cup chopped celery
¼ cup chopped green pepper
1 tablespoon finely chopped onion
3 tablespoons all-purpose flour
1½ cups milk
⅓ cup Wish-Bone *Chunky Blue Cheese
  Dressing*
1 tablespoon chopped pimiento

½ teaspoon salt
Dash pepper
*½ pound flounder fillets, cut into
  bite-size pieces*
*1 package (7 ounces) frozen uncooked
  shrimp, thawed and drained*
*1 package (8 ounces) refrigerated
  buttermilk biscuits*

Preheat oven to 425°F. In medium skillet, melt butter and cook celery, green pepper, and onion until tender. Blend in flour until smooth; gradually add milk, stirring constantly until thickened. Stir in dressing, pimiento, salt, and pepper. Add fillets and shrimp; blend well. Pour into greased 1½-quart casserole; bake 15 minutes. Arrange biscuits on top; bake an additional 10 minutes or until biscuits are golden brown.

Skewered Seafood Boats   *4 servings*

2 medium pineapples
1 cup (8 ounces) Wish-Bone *Russian Dressing*
¼ cup brown sugar
½ teaspoon ground ginger

½ pound uncooked shrimp, cleaned
½ pound scallops
1 large green pepper, cut into chunks
2 cups hot cooked rice
2 tablespoons chopped green onion

Cut pineapples in half lengthwise. Cut fruit from the shells; reserve the shells. Cut fruit into chunks; reserve 1 cup. In small bowl, blend dressing, sugar, and ginger. On skewers, alternately thread shrimp, scallops, green pepper, and reserved pineapple chunks. Grill or broil, turning and basting frequently with dressing mixture, until seafood is done. Meanwhile, wrap tops of reserved shells in aluminum foil; grill cut-side down, or broil, cut-side up, until lightly brown. Remove foil. To serve, combine hot rice with green onion; spoon into reserved shells. Top with skewered mixtures.

Pineapple Chicken Oriental   *4 servings*

Subtly flavored chicken breasts with a succulent filling that will make any dinner a special event.

½ cup Wish-Bone *Italian or Lite Italian Dressing*
1 can (20 ounces) crushed pineapple, drained (reserve liquid)
3 tablespoons brown sugar
½ teaspoon ground ginger

4 whole chicken breasts, skinned, boned, and pounded
⅓ cup finely chopped green pepper
⅓ cup slivered almonds
1 tablespoon cornstarch

In shallow baking dish, combine dressing, reserved pineapple liquid, sugar, and ginger; mix well. Add chicken and marinate in refrigerator, turning occasionally, at least 3 hours. Preheat oven to 375°F. Remove chicken; reserve marinade. In small bowl, combine pineapple, green pepper, and almonds. Spread ¼ pineapple mixture on each chicken breast; roll up and place seam-side down in baking dish. Pour ¼ cup marinade over chicken and bake 35 minutes or until chicken is tender. Remove chicken to heated platter. In small saucepan, combine cooked and reserved marinade with cornstarch; heat, stirring constantly, until slightly thickened, about 2 minutes. Serve over chicken.

Peachy Cornish Hens   *4 servings*

½ cup Wish-Bone *Russian Dressing*
1 can (16 ounces) sliced peaches,
    drained (reserve ¼ cup syrup)

¾ teaspoon ground ginger
2 Cornish hens, split

In large shallow baking dish, blend dressing, reserved syrup, and ginger; add Cornish hens. Cover and marinate in refrigerator, turning occasionally, 4 hours or overnight. Preheat oven to 375°F. Remove hens, reserving marinade. In foil-lined shallow baking pan, place hens skin-side up and bake, basting frequently with reserved marinade, 40 minutes. Add peaches and bake an additional 10 minutes or until hens are done.

Mardi Gras Skillet Chicken   *4 servings*

⅓ cup Wish-Bone *Italian Dressing*
2- to 2½-pound chicken, cut into
    serving pieces
3 cans (8 ounces each) tomato sauce

½ cup chopped onion
1 green pepper, cut into strips
1½ cups uncooked instant rice

In large shallow baking dish, pour dressing over chicken; cover and marinate in refrigerator, turning occasionally, at least 3 hours. In large skillet, brown chicken in marinade. Add tomato sauce, onion, and green pepper; simmer covered 40 minutes or until chicken is tender. Remove chicken and keep warm. To skillet, add rice and cook covered 5 minutes or until rice is tender. Serve with chicken.

Orange-Glazed Chicken   *4 servings*

¾ cup Wish-Bone *Italian Dressing*
½ cup orange marmalade
2 teaspoons ground ginger (optional)

2½- to 3-pound chicken, cut into
    serving pieces

Preheat oven to 350°F. In small bowl, combine dressing, orange marmalade, and ginger. Place chicken, skin-side up, on broiler pan; brush with dressing mixture and bake, basting occasionally, 1 hour or until chicken is tender.

Vegetables

Stuffed Potatoes American *6 servings*

3 medium baking potatoes
¼ cup milk
2 tablespoons butter or margarine
Salt and pepper to taste

⅓ cup Wish-Bone *Chunky Blue Cheese Dressing*
Cooked bacon bits

Preheat oven to 400°F. Bake potatoes until done. While still warm, cut each potato in half lengthwise and scoop out pulp (save shells). In medium bowl, mash potatoes with milk, butter, salt, and pepper; stir in dressing. Refill shells and top with bacon. Bake 15 minutes or until heated through.

Potatoes Parmesan: Use Wish-Bone Italian Dressing and top with grated Parmesan cheese.

Tomato Halves Provençale *8 servings*

2 cups fresh bread crumbs
3 tablespoons finely chopped parsley
2 tablespoons grated Parmesan cheese

½ cup plus 2 tablespoons Wish-Bone *Robusto Italian Dressing*
4 medium tomatoes

Preheat oven to 400°F. In small bowl, combine bread crumbs, parsley, cheese, and ½ cup dressing; set aside. Cut tomatoes in half crosswise; gently squeeze to remove seeds. Place tomato halves, cut-side down, in medium shallow baking dish with remaining 2 tablespoons dressing. Bake 10 minutes. Turn over, then top with bread crumb mixture. Bake an additional 5 minutes or until bread crumb mixture is golden brown.

Sweet 'n Sour Stir Fry   *6 servings*

2 tablespoons oil
1 cup thinly sliced carrots
1 cup snow peas
1 small green pepper, cut into chunks
1 medium tomato, cut into wedges
1 cup sliced water chestnuts

½ cup sliced cucumber, halved
¾ cup Wish-Bone *Sweet 'n Spicy*
    French, Lite Sweet 'n Spicy French,
    Russian, or Lite Russian Dressing
2 tablespoons brown sugar
2 teaspoons soy sauce

In medium skillet, heat oil and cook carrots, snow peas, and pepper over medium heat, stirring frequently, 5 minutes or until crisp-tender. Add tomato, water chestnuts, cucumber, and dressing blended with brown sugar and soy sauce. Simmer 5 minutes or until vegetables are tender. Top, if desired, with sesame seeds.

Crunchy Green Bean Bake   *4 servings*

1 can (16 ounces) green beans, drained
1 jar (2½ ounces) sliced mushrooms,
    drained

⅓ cup Wish-Bone *Chunky Blue Cheese*
    Dressing
Canned French fried onions

Preheat oven to 350°F. In 1-quart casserole, combine all ingredients except onions; bake covered 10 minutes. Top with onions; bake uncovered an additional 5 minutes or until onions are heated.

Hawaiian Sweet Potatoes   *4 servings*

1 can (17 ounces) sweet potatoes,
    drained
¼ cup Wish-Bone *Deluxe French*
    Dressing

1 can (8 ounces) crushed pineapple,
    drained
2 tablespoons shredded coconut
2 tablespoons brown sugar

Preheat oven to 400°F. In medium bowl, mash sweet potatoes; blend in dressing and pineapple. Turn into 1-quart casserole and sprinkle with coconut and brown sugar. Bake 25 to 30 minutes.

Sweet Spicy Glazed Carrots *4 servings*

2 tablespoons Wish-Bone *Sweet 'n Spicy French Dressing*
2 tablespoons brown sugar

1 can (15 ounces) whole carrots, drained

In small skillet, blend dressing with brown sugar; heat until bubbling. Add carrots; cook, stirring constantly, until glazed, about 5 minutes.

Marinated Mushrooms *8 servings*

8 cups water
2 pounds fresh medium mushrooms
2 teaspoons lemon juice

¾ cup Wish-Bone *Italian or Olive Oil Classics Caesar Dressing*

In large saucepan, boil water. Add mushrooms and lemon juice and cook 2 minutes; drain. Toss with dressing; cover and marinate in refrigerator 4 hours or overnight, turning occasionally. Serve with cold meats or poultry, or as an hors d'oeuvre.

Caponata *3½ cups caponata*

½ cup Wish-Bone *Italian or Lite Italian Dressing*
3 cups diced eggplant (about 1 medium)
1 cup sliced celery
½ cup chopped onion

1 can (16 ounces) whole tomatoes, undrained
¼ cup sliced pimiento-stuffed olives
1 tablespoon mashed anchovies
1 tablespoon chopped parsley
1 teaspoon sugar

In large skillet, combine dressing, eggplant, celery, and onion; cook until tender, about 15 minutes. Add tomatoes, olives, anchovies, parsley, and sugar; bring to a boil, then simmer uncovered 15 minutes or until vegetables are tender. Chill. Serve, if desired, with thinly sliced Italian bread.

Beets Hawaiian *4 servings*

1 can (16 ounces) diced beets, drained
1 can (8 ounces) pineapple chunks in natural juice, drained

½ cup Wish-Bone *Russian or Lite Russian Dressing*
¼ teaspoon ground ginger

In medium saucepan, combine all ingredients; heat through. Top, if desired, with shredded coconut.

Glazes, Sauces, & Relishes

Special Summer Barbecue Glaze *2½ cups glaze*

1 envelope Lipton *Onion Recipe Soup Mix*

1 cup (8 ounces) Wish-Bone Sweet 'n Spicy French Dressing
1 jar (12 ounces) apricot preserves

In small bowl, blend onion recipe soup mix, dressing, and preserves. Use as a basting sauce for chicken, spareribs, chops, ham, or other barbecue meats.

Basic Marinade-Barbecue Sauce *1 cup marinade-sauce*

Use as a marinade for steaks and chicken or as a barbecue sauce for hamburgers, frankfurters, spareribs, and chicken.

½ cup Wish-Bone *Italian Dressing*   *½ cup* Wish-Bone *Russian Dressing*

In small bowl, combine ingredients; blend thoroughly.

Sweet-Sour Sauce *1½ cups sauce*

1 cup (8 ounces) Wish-Bone *Deluxe French Dressing*

¼ cup chili sauce
¼ cup pickle relish

Blend dressing with chili sauce and pickle relish. Serve with fish and seafood.

Oriental Relish   *5 cups relish*

½ cup Wish-Bone Sweet 'n Spicy
  French Dressing
¼ teaspoon ground ginger
1 can (8 ounces) crushed pineapple in
  natural juice, drained

1 can (8½ ounces) water chestnuts,
  drained and sliced
1 cup diagonally sliced celery
1 cup diagonally sliced carrots

In medium bowl, blend dressing with ginger. Add pineapple, water chestnuts, celery, and carrots; toss. Cover and chill, tossing relish occasionally, 4 hours or overnight. Store in refrigerator for up to 1 week.

Patio Pepper Relish   *7 cups relish*

4 cups shredded cabbage
1 cup finely chopped green pepper
1 cup finely chopped red pepper
1 cup finely chopped celery

¼ cup finely chopped green onions
⅔ cup Wish-Bone Italian or Lite Italian
  Dressing

In large bowl, combine cabbage, peppers, celery, and green onions; toss with dressing. Cover and marinate in refrigerator, stirring occasionally, 4 hours or overnight. Store in refrigerator for up to 1 week.

Relish for Franks 'n Burgers   *2½ cups relish*

¾ cup Wish-Bone Russian Dressing
1 tablespoon cornstarch
2 to 3 teaspoons dry mustard
1½ cups finely chopped green pepper

1 cup finely chopped cucumber, drained
1 cup finely chopped celery
½ cup finely chopped onion
2 tablespoons chopped pimiento

In small bowl, blend dressing, cornstarch, and mustard. In large saucepan, combine green pepper, cucumber, celery, onion, pimiento, and dressing mixture. Bring to a boil, then simmer 5 minutes, stirring frequently, until mixture is slightly thickened. Spoon into covered container; secure lid and chill. Store in refrigerator for up to 1 week.

Gazpacho Relish *4 cups relish*

1/3 cup Wish-Bone *Italian or Lite Italian Dressing*
1/4 cup tomato sauce
Hot pepper sauce
4 green onions, finely chopped

1 medium green pepper, cut into thin strips
1 medium cucumber, sliced
1 medium tomato, cut into wedges
1 cup diagonally sliced celery

In small bowl, blend dressing, tomato sauce, hot pepper sauce, and green onions. In 1-quart jar, layer green pepper, cucumber, tomato, and celery, adding ¼ dressing mixture between each layer; secure lid tightly and chill, inverting jar occasionally, 8 hours or overnight. Store in refrigerator for up to 1 week.

Calico Corn Relish *4 cups relish*

1/2 cup Wish-Bone *Russian or Lite Russian Dressing*
2 1/2 cups cooked corn

1 cup thinly sliced celery
1/2 cup finely chopped onion
1/4 cup finely chopped pimiento

In large bowl, combine all ingredients. Cover and marinate in refrigerator, stirring occasionally, 4 hours or overnight.

Italian Summer Relish *8 cups relish*

3/4 cup Wish-Bone *Italian Dressing*
1/4 cup dry red wine
1 teaspoon dried basil or 1 tablespoon chopped fresh basil
1 can (20 ounces) chick peas, rinsed and drained (about 2 cups)

2 cups chopped green pepper
1 1/2 cups drained chopped tomato
1 cup sliced celery
1 medium red onion, cut into rings

In large bowl, blend dressing, wine, and basil. Add chick peas, green pepper, tomato, celery, and onion; toss. Spoon into 2-quart jar; secure lid and chill, inverting jar occasionally, 4 hours or overnight. Store in refrigerator for up to 1 week.

Sandwiches and Breads

Reuben Grill   *4 sandwiches*

¹/₃ cup Wish-Bone Thousand Island or
   Lite Thousand Island Dressing
8 slices rye bread
¹/₄ pound sliced Swiss cheese

¹/₄ pound sliced corned beef or roast
   beef
1 can (8 ounces) sauerkraut, drained
2 tablespoons butter or margarine

Spread dressing on bread. On 4 slices, place equal amounts of cheese, beef, and sauerkraut; top with remaining bread. In skillet, melt butter; cook sandwiches in butter until brown on both sides.

—————— ▼▲▼ ——————

Italian Garlic Biscuits   *10 biscuits*

2 cups sifted all-purpose flour
1 tablespoon sugar
2¹/₂ teaspoons baking powder

¹/₂ cup Wish-Bone Italian Dressing
¹/₂ cup milk

Sift flour, sugar, and baking powder into bowl. Stir in dressing and milk until all ingredients are moistened. Preheat oven to 425°F. On floured board, knead dough lightly about 5 to 6 times. Roll dough 1 inch thick and cut with a floured 2-inch biscuit cutter. Place 1 inch apart on ungreased baking sheet and bake 12 to 15 minutes or until biscuits are golden brown.

Italian Parmesan Bread *1 loaf*

¼ cup Wish-Bone *Italian Dressing*
¼ cup soft butter or margarine

¼ cup grated Parmesan cheese
1 loaf (8 ounces) Italian bread

Preheat oven to 375°F. In small bowl, combine dressing, butter, and cheese until well blended. Cut Italian bread in diagonal slices almost through to bottom crust. Spread cut surfaces with dressing mixture. Wrap in foil, partially open at top, and bake for 15 to 20 minutes.

Zesty Beef Salad Rolls *8 servings*

¾ cup Wish-Bone *Creamy Italian*
   Dressing
1 tablespoon horseradish
1½ teaspoons dry mustard
2 cups shredded cabbage

⅔ cup shredded carrot
16 thin slices cooked roast beef (about
   12 ounces)
8 frankfurter rolls

In small bowl, blend dressing, horseradish, and mustard. In medium bowl, combine cabbage, carrot, and ½ cup dressing mixture. Lay 2 slices roast beef side by side, slightly overlapping long sides. Spoon about 3 tablespoons salad mixture along short end of slices; roll jelly-roll fashion. Repeat procedure for remaining slices; chill. Serve on frankfurter rolls and top with remaining dressing mixture.

The Grinder *6 servings*

½ cup Wish-Bone *Italian or Lite Italian*
   Dressing
¼ teaspoon oregano or basil
1 medium tomato, sliced
1 medium red onion, sliced
1 loaf Italian bread, cut in half
   horizontally

¼ pound salami, sliced
¼ pound provolone, Swiss, or Cheddar
   cheese, sliced
¼ pound cooked ham, sliced
½ cup shredded lettuce

In shallow baking dish, pour dressing blended with oregano over tomato and onion. Cover and marinate in refrigerator at least 1 hour. Remove tomato and onion, reserving marinade. On bottom half of bread, layer salami, cheese, ham, tomato, onion, and lettuce. Sprinkle reserved marinade over lettuce and top with remaining bread half.

The Sandwich Loafer   *6 sandwiches*

⅓ cup Wish-Bone *Italian or Lite Italian Dressing*
2 cups shredded cooked chicken or turkey or 1 can (9½ ounces) tuna, drained and flaked
1 small tomato, chopped

½ cup mayonnaise
3 slices bacon, crisp-cooked and crumbled
1 round loaf (about 16 ounces) pumpernickel or rye bread, unsliced
Lettuce leaves

In medium bowl, combine dressing, chicken, and tomato; chill at least 3 hours. Just before serving, blend in mayonnaise and bacon. Cut bread into 12 slices, almost completely through. Fill first slice and then every other slice with chicken mixture; garnish with lettuce. To serve, cut between unfilled slices to form sandwiches.

Barbecued Steak Sandwiches   *8 servings*

½ cup Wish-Bone *Italian or Lite Italian Dressing*
2½- to 3-pound steak (your favorite cut)
½ cup catsup
4 drops hot pepper sauce

1 tablespoon sugar
1 teaspoon dry mustard
2 tablespoons cornstarch
1 cup cold water
Toasted hamburger rolls

In large shallow baking dish, pour dressing over steak. Cover and marinate in refrigerator, turning occasionally, 4 hours or overnight. Remove steak, reserving marinade. In medium saucepan, heat reserved marinade, catsup, hot pepper sauce, sugar, mustard, and cornstarch blended with water. Simmer, stirring occasionally, 5 minutes or until sauce is thickened. Grill or broil steak, turning and basting frequently with sauce, until done. To serve, arrange thinly sliced steak on hamburger rolls and top with remaining sauce.

Vegetable-Cheese Stuffed Loaves *4 servings*

1 pound frozen bread dough, thawed
⅓ cup Wish-Bone *Lite Creamy Italian Dressing*
2 eggs, each beaten separately

2 cups shredded mozzarella cheese (about 6 ounces)
1 medium tomato, chopped
1 medium green pepper, chopped
1 cup broccoli florets

Let bread rise according to package directions. Preheat oven to 375°F. In medium bowl, combine dressing with 1 beaten egg; stir in cheese and vegetables. Divide dough into quarters. On lightly floured board, roll each quarter into 8″ × 8″ square. Along center of each square, equally divide the vegetable mixture. Moisten edges with water; pull edges up, folding and pinching to seal tightly. Place seam-side up on foil-lined 15½″ × 10½″ × 1″ jelly-roll pan. Bake 20 minutes; brush with remaining beaten egg, then bake an additional 10 minutes.

Hearty Hero-Burgers *6 to 8 servings*

¾ cup Wish-Bone *Thousand Island Dressing*
3 pounds ground beef
1½ cups shredded Cheddar cheese
¼ cup finely chopped green pepper

¼ cup minced onion
1 tablespoon parsley flakes
2 teaspoons salt
¼ teaspoon pepper
6 to 8 hero rolls

In large bowl, combine all ingredients except hero rolls. Shape mixture into oblong burgers. Grill or broil until done. Serve in split hero rolls.

Hamburgers Continental *4 servings*

1 pound ground beef
¼ cup Wish-Bone *Italian Dressing*

¼ cup fresh bread crumbs

In medium bowl, combine all ingredients. Shape into patties. Grill or broil until hamburgers are done.

Hamburgers International: Use ¼ cup Wish-Bone Russian Dressing.

Hamburgers Français: Use ¼ cup Wish-Bone Chunky Blue Cheese Dressing.

Vegetable-Cheese Stuffed Loaves

Index